Introduction

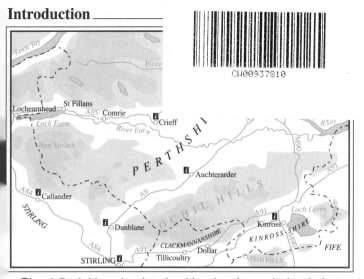

South Perthshire epitomises the old saying about enjoying the best of both worlds, sitting, as it does, right astride the geological Highland Boundary Fault, which technically divides upland from lowland Scotland. This felicitous situation means that the area covered by this book embraces both the truly highland scenery of Loch Earn and Ben Vorlich (*Walk 8*) and the gentle arable land which one passes through between Crieff and Auchterarder.

The routes described here will take the walker to spots where the views outward and beyond the immediate area take in even more marked contrasts: from the summit of Ben Vorlich, for example, can be seen the grander heights of the Lawers range and Ben More and Stobinian, while from the gentle tops of the Ochils can be seen the Forth Bridges, the links of Forth, the petro-chemical complex at Grangemouth and the tower buildings of Cumbernauld!

The cultural and historical contrasts are no less marked: within a few kilometres of one another lie Scotland's ancient capital of Forteviot and the very modern creation that is Gleneagles Hotel and its world-famous golf courses (*16*); the name of the village of St Fillans provides a link back to the time of the Irish-led early Celtic Church, while all around it lie the marks of modernism – water sports, camping and caravan sites, B&Bs and bus parks.

Although the area covered is within easy travelling distance of the major cities, its charm lies in the fact that one can so easily lose oneself in the folds of the varied countryside: as the visitor strolls through the autumn leaves carpeting the paths by the river Lednock (*5,7*), wanders over the little-visited slopes of the Ochils (*18,19*) or sits resting on the edge of Bishop Hill (*20*), high above Loch Leven, it is easy fo imagine that one is very much further away from urban life.

Another variable is, of course, the weather; all four seasons may be encountered in the course of one day – frost, snow, rain, wind, balmy sunshine, soft moonshine and much more – and who would deny that that element of uncertainty and surprise does not add something to the whole experience?

The range of walks covered in this book also represents contrasts: from those which are no more than strolls, such as the Crieff riverside walks (*2,3*), to the journeys, such as the Comrie to Callander through route (*11*), to the ascents, whether modest, as in the case of the Knock at Crieff (*4*) or more ambitious, as in the case of Ben Vorlich and Stuc a' Chroin (*8*).

A guide book is, of course, no more than a beginning, like a first reading book, and the first-time visitor to the area, having sampled the representetive cross-section offered here, should think in terms of returning, emboldened and more adventurous, to seek out on subsequent visits some of the countless other charms of the area.

Enjoy your walking!

Melville Monument, Glen Lednock
(Walks 12,13)

A long walk to the very head of Glenalmond, followed by a comparativley short descent to Loch Tay-side. Very much a walk in and through the hills, yet without any appreciable ascent. Length: **14¹/₂ miles/23km** (one way); *Height Climbed:* **650ft/200m**.

O.S. Sheet 52

Newton Bridge

Newton Bridge lies in the Sma' Glen, at the point where the Hanoverian military road crosses the River Almond (ample parking) and heads across the moors to Amulree and Aberfeldy. It is worth making a detour of a few hundred metres north from Newton Bridge to view the fine old bridge spanning the vigorous little burn just to the west of the road.

The start of the Ardtalnaig route is marked by a right of way sign just a few steps north of Newton Bridge. The estate track leading away from the road continues up the glen for 8 miles/13km; although there are some side turnings, the way on up the glen is always apparent.

The vehicular track eventually gives way to a footpath, but again the way is never in doubt, with the river never more than a few metres away on the left. At the head of the glen, the house at Dunan is a useful target. 300 metres before the house, a three-sided right of way sign by a footbridge indicates the route southwards to Invergeldie, Glen Lednock and Comrie (Walk 5).

At the sheep fanks at Dunan, a further vehicular track is picked up, leading on north-westwards and eventually down to Loch Tay. There are no intermediate turns or difficulties (though there are some

burns to ford), and the upper end of the tarred road is reached ¹/₂ mile/0.75km above Ardtalnaig. For walkers starting from this end, there is a right of way sign at the side of the road.

Please note that Ardtalnaig is some distance from the shops and accommodation, either at Kenmore (7 miles/11km) or at Killin (10 miles/16km).

Eight waymarked routes have been laid out around Crieff (leaflet available from TIC). The following walks use elements from six of them, and you will see their coloured symbols along the routes.
2) *An easy path through the woodland by the Rivers Earn and Turret, with possible extensions up Laggan Hill and to an historic monument.*
Length: **3-7 miles/5-11km**; Height Climbed: **500ft/150m** (on Laggan Hill extension; otherwise negligible). **3)** *A walk past Laggan Hill and by the River Turret, passing Glenturret Distillery on the way.*
Length: **4 miles/6.5km**; Height Climbed: **230ft/70m**. **4)** *A short climb to a fine viewpoint, with possible extensions. Length:* **1/2 mile/1km** *(there and back); Height Climbed:* **230ft/70m**. *It is possible to link elements of these walks to create a longer route around the north of Crieff (see map).*

O.S. Sheet 52

Walk 2) This route starts along the popular riverside path known as Lady Mary's Walk. To reach it, leave James Square by the Comrie road (ie, westwards); at the war memo-

rial in front of the former St Ninian's church, descend to and cross Burrell Street, continue westwards into Milnab Street and follow it all the way downhill to three inter-connect-

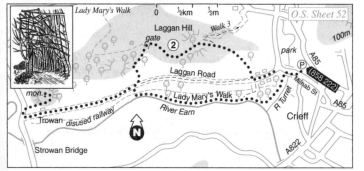

ing parks, Taylor Park, Mungall Park and Macrosty Park. At the car park there is an interpretive board providing information about walks.

The river at the side of the park is the Turret. Cross the road bridge and turn immediately left at a sign indicating Lady Mary's Walk (note also the brown symbol for the Laggan Hill Walk and the blue symbol for the Currochs Walk). This leads downstream, through woodland, past the dismantled arches of the bridge which carried the old Crieff to Comrie railway line, to the confluence of the Turret and the Earn.

The path swings right, by the River Earn. After a short distance it reaches a signposted junction. A turn to the right at this point leads on to the Currochs Walk (*see* Walk 3), but for this walk keep left, signposted for Laggan Road.

Continue along a magnificent avenue of mature beech and oak trees parallel to the river. Follow this for almost a mile/1.5km, with the old railway embankment up to the right

and the river to the left.

The path eventually makes a sharp turn to the right, through the line of the railway at a dismantled bridge, and merges with a cart-track at a T-junction. Here you have a choice:

If you wish to return to Crieff by the quickest route, turn right and follow Laggan Road (marked by orange symbols) back to the start of the walk. **If you would like to visit the splendid hill-top monument to Sir David Baird** (an extension which adds three miles/5km to the walk, there and back), turn left on the path signposted for Strowan Bridge Road (green symbols). A rough but clear path leads between fields, with the monument visible ahead, to the farm at Trowan and the public road just beyond. Turn right along this for a short distance, then right again at a signpost, to reach the monument. Return by the same route.

To continue over Laggan Hill, turn right at the junction, as if returning to Crieff, but then turn left almost immediately on the path signposted for Laggan Hill.

A clear, rough path leads up the slope of the hill then along a flatter section to reach a gate leading onto a track. Turn right along this (signposted for Crieff). There is now a pleasant stretch of walking, along the hill, with views down to Crieff.

At the next signposted junction keep straight ahead (a turn to the left takes you on to Walk 3). Drop down to a four-way junction and turn left. Keep straight ahead at subsequent junctions in the new housing until you reach a T-junction. Turn right here, for a short distance, to return to the start of the walk.

Walk 3) Start this walk as for Walk 2, but at the junction reached just after joining the River Earn turn right, doubling back above the river.

The track passes over the old railway line and continues past new housing to a four-way junction. Go straight on here, following the sign for Laggan Hill (this route is also marked by blue symbols).

Follow a clear track up the slope of the hill for about $^3/_4$ mile/1km to a signposted fork. Keep right here, following the sign for Turretbank Road. After about 50m the main track goes through a gate in a dyke into a field. Turn right just before this (blue symbol) on a narrow footpath running along field edges downhill. After a short distance the main road comes into view.

The path continues towards Currochs Farm. At the bottom of the field, where a gate leads into the

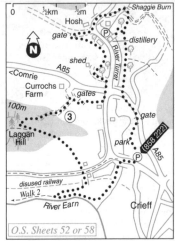

buildings on the left, turn right along the field edge with a hedge to the left. After a short distance there is a kissing gate to the left. Go through this and turn right, along the top of the field. Occasional posts now mark the route across this field and down to a kissing-gate in a fence at the left-hand corner of an area of housing.

Go through this and follow a path behind the houses to the public road. Turn left along this for a short way to reach the main Crieff-Comrie road. Cross this (with care: it can be busy) and walk up the minor road opposite.

After a very short distance turn left onto a farm road signposted for 'The Hosh'. This leads up towards a shed, but you should turn off to the right before reaching it (blue symbol). A further blue symbol, just before a small quarry, points right, leading to a path overlooking the River Turret. This then passes through a gate and continues with a field to the left and beech trees to the right. The distillery and its warehouses are now visible down to the right.

A post points off to the left, leading down to a kissing-gate in a fence. Go through this and turn right, along a clear track, to reach Hosh.

Turn left along the quiet public road and cross the bridge over the river. Walk on past the large house to the right, then turn right on a track signposted for Crieff. This leads to a footbridge by a ford over the Shaggie Burn. Cross this and follow the main track uphill to a signposted junction. Turn right here. After a short distance a signpost indicates the path to a footbridge leading to Glenturret Distillery (Scotland's oldest: it has a shop, restaurant guided tours, etc).

Return to the junction, turn right and follow the paths by the river down to the main road. Cross this (with care) to the pavement on the far side. Turn left for about $^1/_4$ mile/0.5km to reach a metal gate leading into the park by the river. Walk through this to return to the start.

Walk 4) The Knock is the prominent little wooded hill which stands right on the northern edge of Crieff (*see* Crieff area map). Residents at the Hydro Hotel can start the ascent by taking the path immediately opposite the front door of the hotel. Those starting from the centre of the town, should look for Hill Street/Ferntower Road, running from James Square up the side of the Drummond Arms Hotel. Follow this road for some distance until it turns left. This leads towards the Hydro, but turn right at the first junction, leading past stables then behind and above the hotel to a public car park.

From here, an obvious path leads into the woods and up to a lookout point on the western shoulder of the hill. In good conditions, this offers splendid views up Strathearn (*see* below), with pastoral country in the foreground and increasingly rugged hill country beyond. This viewpoint is not the highest point of the hill, which is the twin peak lying some 400m to the north-east. However, that offers no outlook, being simply a cairn of stones in the middle of a circle of enclosing trees.

As well as the direct path up to the viewpoint, there are numerous other paths winding up, over and round The Knock, the most popular being the forestry track which makes a circuit of the hill.

1 Càrn Chòis 2 Glen Turret 3 Ben Chonzie 4 Choinneachain Hill 5 Blue Craigs 6 Stonefield Hill

5 Glen Lednock to Ardtalnaig _____ A

Quite a strenuous walk through the heart of the hills, with some rough going in the middle section. The ascent, however, is accomplished on estate tracks. Good views ahead to the Ben Lawers range. Length: **10 miles/16km** *(one way); Height Climbed:* **1400ft/430m**. *Map and compass necessary.*

O.S. Sheets 51 or 52

This walk starts from the walkers' car park near Invergeldie, about four miles/6.5km along the minor road leading north from Comrie up Glen Lednock. A right of way sign indicates the start of two routes; take the Ardtalnaig route, north from the car park, around the buildings as directed, and onto a stony estate track. Follow this for some 1³/₄ miles/3km, taking care to bear left at the one significant junction (755 290).

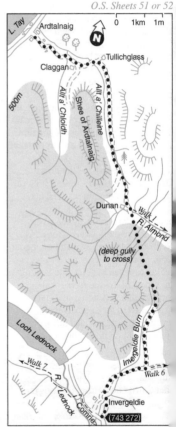

The glen forks near its head. The track keeps to the left and continues climbing, before petering out as it approaches the pass. Continue along a path, which finally loses itself in the wet, peaty terrain on the watershed.

Once over the watershed, a slanting descent leftwards across the hillside will serve. When one comes within sight of the house at Dunan aim for that, and, once well down the hill, aim for the little footbridge over the river some 300m below the house. **In misty conditions, it is essential that walkers be able to use map and compass confidently on this section**.

Once over the footbridge, where there is a triple right of way sign, turn left (upstream) to the house. From this point on, this walk follows the same route as Walk 1.

*As easy an ascent to 3000ft as can be found, with an alternative, more ambitious walk from Glen Turret. Length: **8³/₄ miles/14km** (there and back); Height Climbed: **2300ft/700m**. **Competence with map and compass required.***

O.S. Sheet 52

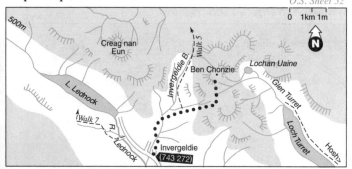

To reach the start-point for the easiest ascent of this hill, follow the directions in Walk 5 to the car park at Invergeldie. From here, start walking as if on Walk 5, following the estate tracks as far as the significant track junction at 755 290. Here, the Loch Tay route branches left and the route towards the summit carries straight on (east). A long slog up the steepest part of the hill takes one eventually to easier ground at the end of the track and to a broad, almost flat southern extension of the hill (772 292). From the end of the track go half-left for ¹/₃ mile/0.5km to join an old fence line along the ridge. Follow this to the summit. The views are extensive; that down Glen Turret towards the Ochils being the best.

If returning by the same route in mist, compass work may be required

to pick up the end of the track, though any descent south-westwards should lead to safety.

There is an alternative approach up Glen Turret, the head of which includes a fine little rugged corrie and corrie-lochan, with encircling crags. The track up the glen can be joined at Hosh (856 237), and passes the Falls of Turret on the way up to Loch Turret. Paths continue by the side of the loch but then peter out, and one has to find one's own way up the steepish and fairly unrelenting eastern slopes of the hill.

The length of this alternative walk is 9 miles/14.5km (one way); the height climbed around 2800ft/850m. The additional use of public transport between Crieff and Comrie and Walk 12 up Glen Lednock would turn this into a good day's expedition.

7 Glen Lednock to Ardeonaig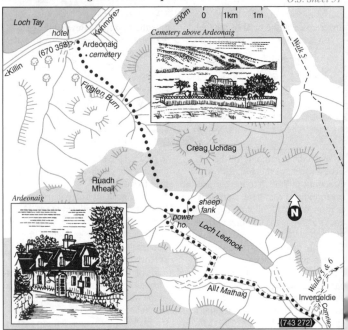

A strenuous hill crossing, with a rough section in the middle coinciding with the ascent. Easy start on tarred (but not public) road. Latterly, good views ahead to the Ben Lawers range. Length: **9½ miles/15km** *(one way, from car park); Height Climbed:* **1450ft/440m**. *Possible loop with Walk 5.* **Navigation skills required**.

O.S. Sheet 51

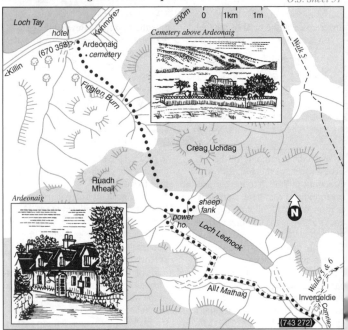

There are two possible starting points for this walk, depending upon how strong you are feeling: either from the village of Comrie, following the first half of the Glen Lednock circuit (Walk 12), and then continuing up the glen road (add 4 miles/6.5km to walk); or, if you are feeling less ambitious, from the walkers' car park near Invergeldie.

From the car park, walk on up the road for another ³/₄ mile/1km to a Y-junction, just before the main road begins to climb. The right of way signpost here indicates the left-hand way, which is still a tarred road.

Although this road gives the appearance of leading up the wrong glen and away from Loch Lednock, it eventually climbs up from the floor of the glen of Allt Mathaig and swings right, over the intervening ridge, to arrive above Loch Lednock about half-way along its length. The road terminates at a gently-humming power house at the head of the loch.

It is tempting to follow the river running into the loch at this point, but this is a mistake; although it appears to lead in the required direction, the river does not offer easy going and ends up in a rock-girt *cul-de-sac*. To proceed, therefore, it is necessary to circle round the head of the loch (fording the River Lednock: tricky if in spate) and to back-track 600m to a circular sheep fank, where one can pick up the old path which used to run along the northern side of the glen before the dam was built.

The old path (little more than a faint sheep path) rises steadily to find a semblance of a shelf running below Creag Uchdag, leading to the slopes above the bealach rather than directly through it. By this time the path has become faint, and one may be as well to steer by the lie of the land or, in bad conditions, on a compass bearing. **Walkers not confident with map and compass are advised not to attempt this route beyond the loch**.

Beyond the bealach, one looks down into the Fin Glen and over the trench of Loch Tay to the Lawers range beyond. The way down the glen is not well defined at first, but

there is little doubt about the route: simply follow one of the vague paths which run down the glen by the burn, always remembering that you will need to be on the east (right-hand) side of the burn further down.

The final descent is through fields, so it is as well to keep an eye open for the gateway in a dyke which helps give the best line. Beyond the gate the route continues along the line of an old track. Follow this to a gate above a black shed by some sheep pens. Go through this, then through another gate to the right of the shed. Drop down below this to join a bulldozed track which leads to a gate in the dyke to the right. Go through this and follow the line of the dyke downhill, past an old cemetery, to reach the public road.

This route was once an important drove road, at a time when Crieff hosted one of the chief cattle fairs, but was superseded by the Glen Ogle route when Falkirk become the principal cattle market. Please note that south Loch Tay has no shops or public transport. The loch is 17 miles/27km long, and Kenmore and Killin are both some distance away. Steamers on the loch once used to call at Ardeonaig, but the modern walker need not expect any such help!

For experienced hill-walkers looking for an alternative return route, Ardtalnaig is 3 miles/5km along the Loch Tay road to the north, from where it is possible to return to the start by reversing Walk 5; a total distance of some $22\frac{1}{2}$ miles/36km.

8 Ben Vorlich / 9 Loch Earn to Comrie_____ A+/A

8) *A steep pull from Loch Earn to the summit of Ben Vorlich; the most southerly of Perthshire's high hills. Length:* **5¹/₂ miles/9km**; *Height Climbed:* **3000ft/900m**. ***Potentially dangerous in adverse conditions.***
9) *A long, lineal hill walk crossing a low pass. The path is indistinct in places:* **map and compass required**. *Length:* **15 miles/24km** *(one way); Height Climbed:* **1800ft/550m**.

O.S. Sheets 51 & 57

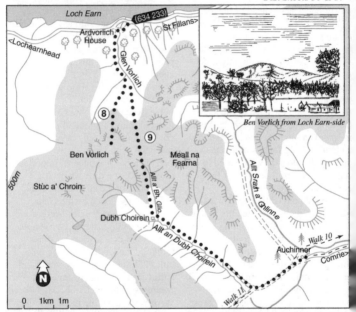

Ben Vorlich from Loch Earn-side

Walk 8) Ben Vorlich is the principal peak of Southern Perthshire, in terms both of height and of visual prominence. If first-time visitors to the area climb nothing else, then they will go home with one of Perthshire's major hill-walks under their belts.

While the more adventurous climber may choose to approach from the south, from Callander or from Comrie, the first-timer should take the established path from the minor road along the south side of Loch Earn. Informal parking areas are available at the loch-side, near Ardvorlich House, 5 miles/8km from St Fillans.

The route towards the hill starts at the little hump-backed bridge near the back drive (east drive), and small direction-signs ('hill walkers') steer walkers past the farm and the main house. Other notices request that bikes should not be taken, dogs should be kept on leads and walkers should follow the marked paths at times when estate activities are likely to be in progress.

The first ascent above the house is on a vehicular track, which splits after a mile/1.5km, with the track to the right leading on up the hill and that to the left heading up Glen Vorlich (Walk 9).

Go right. After 1/2 mile/1km, having crossed a footbridge and left the trees, the route becomes a foot-path only (though greatly improved in recent years). A long pull commences, leading up through grassy and heathery terrain to the prominent and obvious north ridge. This runs straight to the summit dome, at which point the route swings left for a short distance to reach the summit. There are steep and potentially dangerous flanks to this mountain, though the summit visitor need never be near them. The actual summit area is in the form of a short east-west ridge, with a trig point at the west end and a shelter cairn at the east end.

Ben Vorlich's twin, Stùc a' Chroin, lies a mile/1.5km away to the south-west, but the walker of modest experience should note that steep and broken ground separates the two, plus a considerable descent/re-ascent.

Return by the same route. If leaving the summit in misty conditions, please remember that you must steer north-west for a short distance from the trig point, down screes, before swinging right along the line of the north ridge.

Walk 9) For the path to Comrie, start as above but keep left, up Glen Vorlich, at the junction.

This is a rough vehicular track, which becomes rougher. Watch out for a point where the track swings left and the pedestrian path separates from it (marked by a plain wooden stake). In clear conditions, the little pass for which one is aiming (638 185) will already be apparent, under the steep eastern flanks of Ben Vorlich.

The path is wet and faint in places, and walkers should be capable of setting a compass bearing to reach the pass. Thereafter, the first mile/1.5km southwards is down a well-defined little glen, though the going is wet and the path is intermittent.

At the ruins at Dubh Choirein a path cuts right towards Callander. For this route, however, cross Allt a' Bhealaich Gliogarsnaiche (you may find it easier to cross earlier if it is in spate) and continue down the glen on an improving path (later track). Follow this for a further 2 1/4 miles/3.5km to join Walk 11 by the bridge over Allt an Dubh Choirein. Turn left and continue until you reach the end of the public road, then follow the directions given in Walk 10 to reach Comrie.

10) *A low-level loop through the pleasant woodland of the glen. Length:* **up to 15 miles/24km**; *Height Climbed:* **up to 300ft/90m**. **11)** *A modest hill-crossing, providing good views of the lesser-known side of Ben Vorlich and an attractive diversion to Bracklinn Falls. Length: (Comrie to Callander)* **15 miles/24km**; *Height Climbed:* **1300ft/400m**. *Length:* *(road-end to road-end)* **5 miles/8km**; *Height Climbed:* **1600ft/180m**.

O.S. Sheet 57

Bridge over the River Earn, Comrie

Walk 10) Glen Artney runs south-west into the hills south of Comrie. To reach it on foot, walk south from

the centre of the village on the B827, turning right onto a minor road a little under a mile/1.5km from the end of the houses. This road is usually very quiet, and provides pleasant walking up the southern side of the glen.

It is possible simply to retrace your steps, but there is also an alternative return on tracks along the northern side of the glen. To join this, either cross the Water of Ruchill at the bridge below Dalchruin (*see* map: this cuts 3 miles/5km from the total distance), or continue until the road crosses the river. Just beyond the bridge go right over a stile and cross a field to a bridge over Allt Srath a' Ghlinne to join the track beyond.

Either way, the track crosses a bridge over a tributary just east of the bridge below Dalchruin. A little over a mile/1.5km beyond this the main track swings left to climb to Blairmore. At this point turn right onto a fainter track which quickly passes through a gate. There is one further fork in the track, about a mile/1.5km further on. Keep right here and continue to join a metalled road at Dalrannoch. Follow this back into Comrie.

The walk down the northern side of the glen, with its fine birch woods, is much to be recommended.

Walk 11) The hill-crossing to Callander can be started on foot from Comrie along either of these routes up Glen Artney. Alternatively, the route can be shortened by driving to the parking place a short distance from the end of the public road.

Whether you have arrived by car or on foot, continue to the white gate at the end of the public road (693

154), just beyond which there is a right of way sign for the start of the route to Callander, pointing towards a steeply-rising track leading up the slopes to the south-west.

There is only one junction, and that is just over a mile/1.5km ahead, at Allt an Dubh Choirein. From this spot, it should be possible to obtain good views of the steepest and grandest sides of Ben Vorlich and Stùc a' Chroin (*see* Walk 8). This is also the point at which Walk 9, from Loch Earn, joins from the right. For this route, however, cross the bridge over the burn and continue west-south-west.

Shortly, one crosses – imperceptibly – out of Perthshire and into Stirlingshire. About a mile/1.5km beyond the highest point on the track, and after going through a gate some 400m before the buildings at Arivurichardich, it is possible to make a short cut down to the left of the track to the floor of the glen and a bridge over the Keltie Water. Thereafter, the track continues in a generally southerly direction, reaching the tarred road shortly after Braeleny Farm.

Follow this for 2 miles/3km to Callander. Shortly before the town is reached there is a car park to the left of the road, and a $1/2$ mile/1km path leading to the Bracklinn Falls.

Beyond the car park, the road passes the approach to the golf course, crosses the old railway bridge and descends to the eastern end of the main street.

Walks South Perthshire

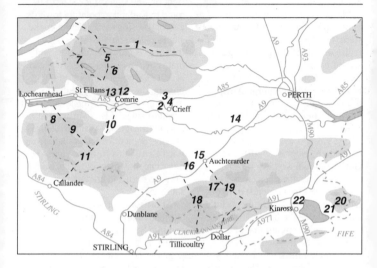

Grades

A+ ... Full walking equipment – including map and compass – and previous hill walking experience essential

A ...... Full walking equipment required

B ...... Strong footwear and waterproof clothing required

C ...... Comfortable footwear recommended

NB: Assume each walk increases at least one grade in winter conditions, **A** and **A+** routes becoming extremely treacherous.

— www.pocketwalks.com —

Published by: Hallewell Publications, The Milton, Foss, Pitlochry, Perthshire PH16 5NQ
Printed by: Thomson Litho Ltd, East Kilbride

While every care has been taken in the preparation of this guide, the publishers cannot accept responsibility for any loss, damage or injury resulting from its use.

Walks South Perthshire

walk	grade
1 Newton Bridge to Ardtalnaig	A
2 Laggan Hill Walk	B
3 Currochs Walk	B
4 The Knock	C
5 Glen Lednock to Ardtalnaig	A
6 Ben Chonzie	A
7 Glen Lednock to Ardeonaig	A
8 Ben Vorlich	A+
9 Loch Earn to Comrie	A
10 Glen Artney	B
11 Comrie to Callander	A
12 Lower Glen Lednock Circuit	B
13 Maam Road Walk	B
14 Roman Road & Signal Stations	C
15 Auchterarder: Provost's Walk	C
16 Gleneagles to Blackford	C
17 The Frandy Reservoirs	B
18 Blackford to Tillicoultry	A
19 Auchterarder to Dollar	A
20 Bishop Hill	B
21 Kinnesswood	C
22 Loch Leven Shoreline	C

Gentle riverside and woodland walks within reach of Comrie's hotels and tearooms. Some steps and some wet going underfoot. Waterfall viewing platforms. Possibility of a short, steep extension. Length: **4 miles/6.5km**; *Height Climbed:* **350ft/100m**.

O.S. Sheet 52

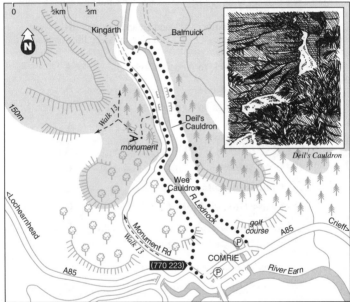

Deil's Cauldron

This walk offers a delightful 'closed circuit' through woodland and riverside terrain, starting and finishing within the body of the village of Comrie. There are two convenient car parks, from each of which the circuit is signposted: one is at the east end of the village, immediately east of the old railway bridge; the other is towards the west end of the village, half way along the north-south section

of the main road, between the two prominent right-angled turns.

The signs for the circuit are the standard white lettering on green background style used by Perth & Kinross Council. The following description follows a clockwise circuit, starting from the second of the two car parks mentioned above.

Follow the main road for a little more than 100m to the second of the two right-angled bends, but go straight on, up the first few metres of Monument Road. At a pair of 'abandoned' high stone gate posts, look out for the first sign and turn right into a leafy track.

After a few minutes of level going, this swings left and begins to climb gently. First the sound of the river, below and to the right, becomes apparent, then, as the gorge narrows, one begins to obtain glimpses of tumbling water and wet rocks. The going all the way is on leaf-strewn, earthy – sometimes muddy – paths, through mixed woodland of birch, oak and beech.

The signpost at the start indicated the destination as being the 'Deil's Cauldron', but one comes first to the Wee Cauldron, which is indicated by a wooden knee-high sign, pointing to the right and onto a loop of path which goes down to the very edge of the gorge, where there is a viewing platform. There are steps, fences and guard rails which ensure that the viewer is completely safe.

Back on the main path, one senses that the gorge is narrowing further still, and the path becomes squeezed between the road above and the river below. The approach to the Deil's Cauldron is 'furnished' with further board walks, fences and steps, which take one right into the throat of the gorge, and close to the falling water and attendant noise.

The onward path climbs up to road level and eventually onto the road. After 100m one has the choice of adding an extra spur to the walk by climbing the steep little path up to the prominent obelisk of Lord Melville's Monument. To continue the main circuit, however, follow the road out of the woods and onwards for some 400m to a Y-junction (road left, track right), where a further sign indicates the way down to the riverside and a bridge. This is the half-way point on the circuit. The route back down is of a different character, being high above the river and for the most part out of sight of it. The surrounding woodland offers ever-changing scenes, with the odd clearing and view-point giving prospects over the surrounding countryside.

Any path junctions are signed and one arrives back at village level at the east end car park. The footbridge over the river leads to a pedestrian route back along the northern fringe of the village to the west end car park and the starting point.

1 *Ben Halton* 2 *Beinn Dearg* 3 *Mór Bheinn* 4 *Ben Vorlich* 5 *Beinn Fuath* 6 *Loch Earn* 7 *Little Port Hill* 8 *The Girron* 9 *Creag Liath*

13 Maam Road Walk _____ B

A pleasant circuit on paths of varying quality through woodland and over the open hill. Length: **6 miles/9.5km**; *Height Climbed:* **650ft/ 200m**. *Fine views from Lord Melville's Monument. Grazing animals; please keep dogs on leads.*

O.S. Sheet 52

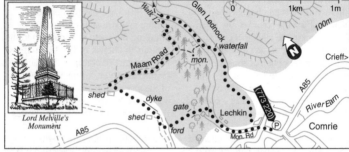

Lord Melville's Monument

Start as for Walk 12, but when the Glen Lednock path goes between the gate posts keep straight on up Monument Road. Pass through the buildings at Lechkin and turn left at the second signpost for Kindrochet (note purple symbol for walk).

Follow the boggy path through the wood to reach a gate in a dyke at its far end. Cross this and continue across the field beyond with a bank of gorse up to the right (a post in the middle of the field marks the way.)

At the far side of the field cross a shallow ford and turn right up a clear track (signposted Kindrochet). Follow this up to a tin-roofed shed and turn left beyond, with a dyke to the right and a field down to the left.

Follow this dyke across the hill, passing through gates as necessary, to reach another tin-roofed shed. Turn right here (signposted Maam Road)

on a clear track climbing up and across the slope. After a short way a faint path cuts off to the left, just before a bridge over a small burn. Ignore this path and continue on the main track, which is quite clear up to the watershed before Glen Lednock.

At this point a sign indicates the start of a path heading through the conifers to the right. Here you have a choice: either **a)** turn right to reach the Melville Monument (*see* Walk 12 for view), beyond which the path drops steeply to the Glen Lednock road; or **b)** carry straight on; dropping down the open hillside to join the road above the woods.

In either case, turn right having reached the road. Just beyond the foot of the monument path turn left at the sign for the Glen Lednock Circular Walk and follow the clear paths by the river back to Comrie.

*Easy, almost level walking, with historical interest thrown in, through
a mixture of woodland and open country with occasional fine views.
Length:* up to **6 miles/9.5km** (there and back, walking both sections)*;
Height Climbed:* negligible. *No dogs.*

O.S. Sheet 58

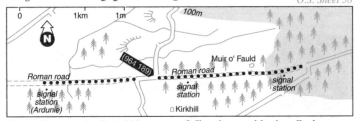

For the Romans, the Gask Ridge,
running west from Perth along the
northern edge of Strathearn, was of
strategic importance. Not only did it
carry a road between their major base
at Braco and the River Tay, it also
provided a vantage point overlooking
a large area, from the Ochils in the
south to the highland edge.

Most of the Roman road has been
incorporated into the modern road
system, but a short section can still
be explored on foot. To reach it,
drive north from Auchterarder on the
B8062. Immediately after crossing
Kinkell Bridge (over the River Earn)
turn right. Pass through Trinity Gask
then turn left, passing the church.
Park by the sign for Ardunie Fort.

The section can be divided into
two parts: **1)** a 1¹/₂ mile/2.5km stretch
through woodland (easy but limited
parking at both ends; NB – leave field
access unobstructed!), which gives
access to two signal stations, Muir o'
Fauld and Kirkhill, and **2)** a 1¹/₂ mile/

2.5km there-and-back walk along an
easy track, giving access to Ardunie
signal station. All three stations lie
on the south side of the road; NB
– Kirkhill lies a little way back in the
trees and is not immediately obvious;
however, it is the best picnic site of
the three, with good views to the
south over Strathearn and the Ochils.

Although the stations can only
be identified by the outline of their
foundations, there is, at all three sites,
an Historic Scotland information
board showing how the stations
would have looked and giving some
of the history of the period.

The walking is for the most
part easy and almost level, modern
farm-tracks having adopted the
line of the Roman road. The 300m
section immediately west of the
ruined Muir o' Fauld Farm consists
of unmanaged rough woodland and
does not look particularly inviting. A
little perseverance will take walkers
through this to easier going beyond.

15 Auchterarder: Provost's Walk _____ C

A fine network of village walks, allowing an outer loop taking in the maximal route and also permitting many options for extending or shortening the complete circuit. Views of the Ochils, the Strathearn farmlands and Ruthven Water. Length: **4 miles/6.5km***; Height Climbed:* negligible.

O.S. Sheet 58

Auchterarder is remarkably well supplied with walks just on the very fringe of the town, the main 'outer circuit' being known as 'The Provost's Walk'. Many of the segments of the network still retain their colourful old, everyday local names, such as Oak Walk, Townhead

Walk, Shepherd's Wynd, Johnny Matthew's Road, John Moir's Park, Beggarmuir Road and others. From the south side of the main street, there are several closes which run between the buildings and out into the fields lying between the town and the Ruthven Water to the south, and these offer easy means of leaving the built-up area and quickly reaching the river.

Although the circuit can be done from any point, either in its entirety or in parts, the best place to start is at Western Road Park, on the main road near the western edge of the town. Here there is a large information board at the entrance to the park, showing a map and the various routes.

Follow the eastern (townward) edge of the park (known as Quarry Road), past the football pavilions and the civic amenity site, down an open grassy slope to an area of trees close to the bypass road (A9). Just before the fence bordering the road, turn left, parallel to the bypass, and along one of the obvious paths leading back towards the town, with fields on the left and the main road just beyond the hedge and fence to the right. Ignore other links back up to the town and continue to the bottom end of a *cul-de-sac* (Ruthven Street), at a point where the Ruthven Water appears from under the A9.

Here, there is the option of passing under the road and so accessing a further network of routes to the south. To continue the circuit, however, keep to the left of the river. Of the two paths ahead, take that further from the river. This leads, in 400m or so, to a group of houses at West Mill, then, by the Ladeside Walk, to the foot of Abbey Road (a turn to the right here, across the bridge over the A9, leads onto the start of the long hill walk to Dollar: *see* Walk 19). Go through the yard at Glenruthven Mill, where there is another display board showing all the local walks. Beyond the buildings, a clear path – the Common Loan – rises straight ahead and almost immediately swings left and uphill, between fields and back to the main street – called Feus at this point – near its lower (eastern) end.

Turn left along the main street, passing the end of the B8062 Crieff road (Hunter Street) and continuing along High Street. Walk through the centre of the town and watch for Castleton Road cutting off to the right. Turn right here and follow this road, out of the town, for about half a mile/1km.

This leads to Castleton, where a broad vehicular track heads off to the left from the public road signposted for Lower Borland Farm. Turn onto this. 600m ahead, this appears to run straight to a house, but divert left just before the house, through a small gate and onto a pedestrian path. Continue to a stile and turn left into a strip of woodland. The path through the trees – The Oak Walk – winds gently uphill, between fields at first, and eventually terminates amongst houses on Tullibardine Road.

Turn left to follow Tullibardine Road then Orchil Road back towards the town centre and to the start of the circuit at Western Road Park (pavements all the way). *En route*, one passes a memorial cairn marking Queen Victoria's Diamond Jubilee in 1897.

A delightful walk with mixed scenery, including the Gleneagles Hotel and golf courses and panoramas along the northern flank of the Ochils. Possible refreshments at Blackford before returning. Length: **4 miles/ 6.5km** (there and back); Height Climbed: negligible.

O.S. Sheet 58

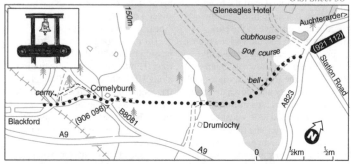

From the main entrance to Gleneagles Hotel (easy parking at Station Road, beside the golf practice area), go south some 50m along the A823, to a broad entrance onto the golf course, from which a red gravel track winds its way across the course. This is used by horse-riders and others, and walkers need have no fear of interrupting play. It is wise, however, to keep an eye open for golfers and to be prepared to wait while they play.

The red track climbs to a group of pines and firs; carry straight on here, ignoring a right-hand fork. Beyond the trees, the track curls round a hillock and descends to an ancient ship's bell, which serves as an 'all clear' to golfers approaching a blind green. A few steps beyond the bell, leave the red track and turn right onto the golfers' concrete 'buggy track'

and follow it through a strip of larch trees. Look across the fairway ahead and to the left and identify, close to a clump of mature beech trees, a pair of metal gates in the fence bordering the course. To reach these, follow paths (some concrete, some gravel) round the back of the green, bearing left at each junction.

Leave the course through the little pedestrian gate. From here on, the route follows a delightful grassy track along the edge of the woodlands on the right, with changing views of the Ochils to the left. There are no junctions and, beyond the woods, the track leads down through an open grassy area towards a farm, skirts the near edge of it and so to a wooden gate and an exit onto the public road a few hundred metres from Blackford.

Return by the same route.

A simple walk into the heart of the Ochils range, with the advantage of tarmac all the way (not a public road). A fine mixture of hill and water scenery, with the option of more ambitious additions if desired. Length: **5 miles/10km** *(there and back); Height Climbed:* **360ft/110m**. *Possible link with Walk 18.*

O.S. Sheet 58

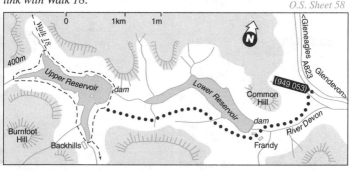

A Water Board tarred road offers the means of penetrating right to the heart of the Ochils without getting one's feet wet, though it should be noted that this road is not open to the public to drive up. This understanding operates on trust; please respect it.

The start is just off the A823 Glen Devon to Gleneagles road, at a conspicuous railing-lined turn-off a short distance south of the watershed. Turn in here: there is room to park on the left, 100m beyond the cattle grid.

The way ahead is clear; one passes a fish farm by the side of the River Devon and shortly afterwards the grassy slope of the first dam wall comes into sight. The road zig-zags up and past the dam, and leads to a pleasant level stretch of walking not far from the waters of the lower

reservoir. A second ascent takes one high above the reservoir, with views ahead to the high hills in the centre of the range and the dam wall of the upper reservoir ¹/₂ mile/1km or so ahead.

Having arrived there, one can simply retrace one's steps, but there are other possibilities as well:

One may cross the dam wall, either just for the stroll and the view or as the first part of a walk right round the reservoir (3¹/₂ miles/5.5km, wet feet!); or one may link up with Walk 18 (*see* map); or one may use the reservoir as an 'advance base' for an ascent of Ben Cleuch (903 006), the highest point in the Ochils (3¹/₂ miles/5.5km from the dam, no path. Map and compass proficiency necessary).

A traverse across the spine of the Ochils range, rising to 1750ft/540m and passing not far from the range's highest top, Ben Cleuch. Superb outward views to the highland hills and south over the Clackmannanshire lowlands and the Forth. **Length: 9 miles/14km** (one way); **Height Climbed: 1400ft/430m.** ***Some navigation required.***

O.S. Sheet 58

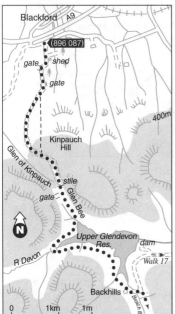

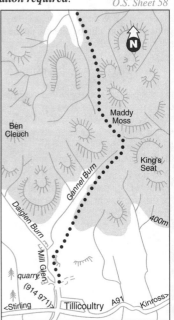

The original path end in Blackford is now cut off by the new A9. It is still possible to start the walk from Blackford – leaving the village at its west end and crossing the dual carriageway to join a minor road running parallel to the main road – but the traffic can be fierce. It may be better to start either from the parking place to the south of the A9, or from the minor road itself.

Walk east along the minor road. Shortly, a right of way sign will be found, indicating the start of the route. A track leads directly towards the hills. At a junction by a shed a track cuts off to the left. Ignore this and carry straight on, following the track up to a stand of conifers. Swing right in front of the trees (ignoring the track turning left at their far end), then left just beyond (there is a gateway to the right at this point).

The track climbs to a gateway. Go through this and turn right. After a short distance there is a plank bridge over the ditch to the left. The original path, now faint, climbs directly up the hill from here; alternatively, one can follow the vehicular track round the shoulder of the hill and up the Glen of Kinpauch. Just before the pass at the head of the glen the main track doubles back to the left. Cross a stile here and continue on an old path to the pass. There is a gate to the right here: ignore this and walk on down the left-hand (east) side of Glen Bee.

The glen ends within ¹/₂ mile/1km, its lower reaches having lain beneath Upper Glendevon Reservoir since the 1950s. Upon reaching the reservoir, descend right to an obvious stile and follow the shore to a bridge over the River Devon. Climb the bank beyond to a stile, turn left, parallel to the fence round the reservoir, and continue until the shore bends right by the southern 'creek' of the reservoir. Cross a stile by a gate then cross a field to another stile. Cross the steep valley of the Muckle Burn and another stile just beyond, then contour round to a further stile below Backhills Farm. Cross a field to reach the bridge over the Broich Burn.

Turn right beyond the bridge and walk south for 250m, crossing two burns, then turn left, just before a sheep pen, and climb the steep grassy slope to join the obvious ATV (all terrain vehicle) track on the flat ground above. This leads all the way to the main backbone of the Ochils, at a height of 540m, at an area known as Maddy Moss. The col (923 010) is crossed by a fence marking the Perthshire/Clackmannanshire boundary, and the best line is marked by an old iron stile set into the fence.

Navigation over this higher part of the route is difficult in misty conditions, and walkers attempting the route should be confident of their compass work. Beyond the stile, follow a fence which leads ahead to a wet depression to the north-west of King's Seat. Cross this depression and pick up a path running south-west above the deep glen running in the same direction: the Gannel Burn. Following the burn is tedious; the path is much to be preferred.

Once found, this path descends steadily for some 1¹/₄ miles/2km in very nearly a straight line. Descending towards the junction between the Gannel Burn and its neighbour, the Dalglen Burn, the path gradually swings round the shoulder of the hill (ie, to the left) and so onto the open grassy slopes above Tillicoultry, with the town's quarry visible to the right. A gate gives access to a path through the trees bordering the gorge and so to the edge of the town at the top of Upper Mill Street. A few metres down this street is the Woolpack Inn, where thirsts may be quenched.

A traverse right through the Ochils range, with one significant – but long and gentle – ascent to a pass at 1450ft/440m. Good outward views to Strathearn and the highland hills. Dramatic finish at Dollar Glen. Refreshment facilities mid-way, at Glen Devon. Length: **11 miles/18km** (one way)*; Height Climbed:* **1400ft/420m**. *No dogs.*

O.S. Sheet 58

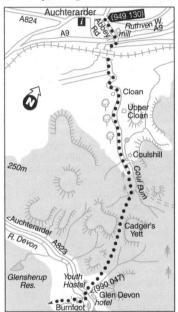

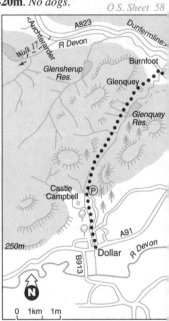

From the lower part of the main street in Auchterarder, follow Abbey Road down to and across the Ruthven Water. Continue across the bridge over the A9 and turn right at the T-junction. After 400m this minor road bends south and climbs to Cloan, Upper Cloan and Coulshill (979 093), where the public road ends, and by

which point one has already climbed to a height of 230m. There is a right of way sign here, indicating the true start of the route, and the tarmac gives way to rough earth and stones.

The track passes two stands of conifers. Just beyond the second it crosses a bridge over a substantial burn and swings uphill (right). The surface now changes to pleasant short turf between the ruts of the track. Looking ahead, one can see the nick in the skyline where one is heading; looking back, broad vistas of Strathearn and the highland hills are already beginning to open out. The track twists its way upwards, wet in places but always discernible, to pass through a gate in the little pass at a height of 440m. This spot (987 073) is known as 'The Cadgers' Yett', as it was the route taken across the hills by the travelling packmen of old.

From here, the highest point of the day, the route descends by easy gradients over delightful short turf towards Glen Devon. After the gates at the start of the enclosed land, keep left (downhill) towards the prominent buildings below.

Turn left and follow the road for 200m, looking out for another right of way sign on the right, pointing down to and over the river. [If refreshments are desired, continue past this sign for a further 100m to the Tormaukin Hotel.] From the sign, cross the bridge and the river, and head half-right by a small footpath, which leads, in one field's length, to a group of houses at Burnfoot. Once through the gate there, turn right over a stone bridge then left immediately beyond.

Leave Burnfoot by a gateway and follow a grassy track diagonally uphill to the right, marked by a yellow arrow on a post. The path passes through a gate in a deer fence and enters an area of new planting before forking. Keep left, continuing

on the same line, to reach a level track above. Turn left along this. After 600m go through another gate in the deer fence and stay right of a stock fence to bypass Glenquey Farm. At the far end of the field go over a stile on the left and rejoin the track, which soon passes through another gate in the deer fence.

The track leads past Glenquey Reservoir and on through the obvious little pass beyond. Easy walking leads shortly to the highest point of this section of the route, where a wooden kissing-gate takes one into the forest on the left. At this point one passes out of Perthshire (one of the largest counties in Scotland) into Clackmannanshire (the smallest).

The way leads gently downhill and, beyond the forest, emerges just above Castle Campbell, the easternmost stronghold of what is generally thought of as a west-coast clan. From here, the views southwards take in the lowlands of Clackmannanshire and the serpentine twists of the River Forth below Stirling. From the car park at the end of the public road, there is a choice of descending past the castle and through the gorge or, more directly but less interestingly, down the road. Both routes lead to 'The Burnside' – particularly attractive in spring, when there is a profusion of pink blossom on the cherry trees. At the foot of The Burnside one reaches Dollar's main street, where there are tea rooms and hotels. Dollar is on the St Andrews to Stirling bus route.

20) *A moderate hill walk, rewarded with superb views over Loch Leven and to the nearby Lomonds of Fife; track for much of the way, with some rough heather and grass on the descent.* Length (full circuit)*:* **8 miles/ 13km***; Height Climbed:* **1000ft/300m***.* Length (up and back)*:* **6 miles /10km***; Height Climbed:* **830ft/250m***.* **21)** *A short, low-level loop through farmland and woodland overlooking Loch Leven.* Length: **3 miles/5km***; Height Climbed:* **250ft/70m***.*

O.S. Sheet 58

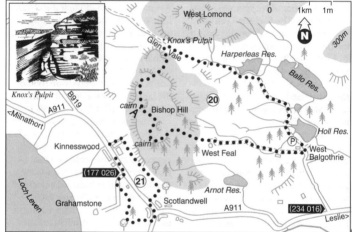

Walk 20) Although Bishop Hill sits a short distance inside Kinross-shire, the best starting point for the ascent, giving a dramatic last-minute view of Loch Leven, lies just into Fife. From the A911 road 1½ miles/2.5km west of Leslie, turn north up a Water Board road, marked by a right of way signpost, and park at the road-end at Holl Reservoir.

Retrace your steps to the last crossroads (225 032, brown wooden signpost) and turn right (west). A long straight farm track climbs gradually, passing West Feal Farm on its right (north) side, then leading more steeply up into a belt of trees. Above the trees, a grassy cart track leads on but swings gradually right (north-west). The line to the summit lies more to the left, keeping parallel to the wall and the forest edge on the left. In misty conditions these may be relied upon to lead to the summit.

The last steps to the cairn should produce a sudden unfolding of the dramatic view ahead, little guessed-at from the somewhat ordinary ascent. Loch Leven, with its islands and castle, lies spread out below, with the natural basin of Kinross-shire extending beyond it and westwards. Watch also for gliders, which often fly along the face of the hills.

The easiest return is by a direct retracing of the steps, but a slight extra effort opens up the option of a delightful airy walk along the edge of the western slopes. From the cairn, look north along the edge of the hills. Another hill topped by a cairn is visible. Follow the grassy cart-track which, running a little way behind the edge of the hills, heads roughly towards the cairned hill. Immediately after passing through a dyke, the track splits. Keep left here and continue to reach a gate. Cross this: the way up the hill is clear from this point.

If you wish to continue the circular route, follow the path which runs on along the edge of the hills until it reaches a dyke/fence crossed by a stile. Turn right here and follow the line of the wall, passing a scattered group of wind-blown larches on the way, to a gate at a junction of dykes. Turn left beyond this and follow a path downhill to a gate leading on to the main track

through Glen Vale. Turn right along this.

The route now becomes a tour of the reservoirs. The first mile/1.5km, towards Harperleas Reservoir, is on a grassy/muddy path. Just before Harperleas, go through a wooden kissing-gate on the right (south) and join a gravel Water Board track. 400m along this track there is a junction, with a signposted path heading off to the right. Ignore this and follow the main track all the way back to the car park at Holl Reservoir.

Walk 21) For the short route, park in Kinnesswood – in the western lee of Bishop Hill – and walk beyond the south-eastern end of the village. After a short distance an arrow points right, down a clear track. Thereafter, the route – designated the 'Tetley Tea Trail' – is well signposted; leading through farmland and woodland to Scotlandwell, then returning to the start through the scattered woodland on the face of the Lomond Hills.

The one gap in the signposting is in Scotlandwell itself. To find the correct route, walk out of the village up the west road. After a short distance an arrow points up the slope to the right, after which the route is quite clear, with waymarkers leading to the eastern edge of Kinnesswood.

1 Benarty Hill **2** St Serf's Island **3** Kinnesswood **4** Cleish Hills **5** Castle Island **6** The Ochils **7** Kinross

A short walk providing fine views. Easy walking on made paths, past golf course, fields and lochside, finishing at Burleigh Sands. Length: **1½ miles/2.5km** (one way)*; Height Climbed: none.*

O.S. Sheet 58

To find the start, follow the main street in Kinross to very nearly the north end of the town, and look out for a short street called Sunnypark on the right (east side), recognisable by the small red-sandstone cottage on the corner. A green and white walker's sign also marks the start, but it has its back to the centre of the town!

Almost immediately, a wooden kissing-gate on the left leads onto an earthen path through trees and alongside a burn; one passes the last of the houses and the path leads through an area of waste ground, soon reaching a gap in a stone wall leading onto the golf course. A wooden sign here indicates a sharp left turn, and the path follows an attractive line of mature beech trees along the side of the course. There are good views ahead to Bishop Hill and over the Fife boundary to West Lomond.

This path leads naturally to an impressive iron gate taking one through the wall and off the course. SNH signs here indicate that one is entering the Loch Leven National Nature Reserve. Turn right through a wooden swing gate onto a fenced path along the margin between the loch-side reeds and the nearby fields, crossing the North Quiech Burn by an arched wooden bridge.

The path leads directly to an area of pine trees close to the shore at Burleigh Sands, a popular paddling and picnic spot. The path turns left here, quickly reaching a footbridge over a small burn. A turn to the right here links with a path running a little further behind the shore. Alternatively, if you keep straight on you will quickly reach a small car park amongst the pines.

1 West Lomond **2** Bishop Hill **3** Loch Leven **4** Benarty Hill